THE 21st CENTURY ADMINISTRATIVE LEADER

THE 21st CENTURY ADMINISTRATIVE LEADER

SARAVANAN SATHIYASEELAN

PARTRIDGE
A Penguin Random House Company

ISBN: Hardcover   978-1-4828-5262-2
             Softcover   978-1-4828-5261-5
             eBook   978-1-4828-5263-9

To order additional copies of this book, contact
Toll Free 800 101 2657 (Singapore)
Toll Free 1 800 81 7340 (Malaysia)
orders.singapore@partridgepublishing.com

www.partridgepublishing.com/singapore

CONTENTS

Dedicated to my soul mate – Ramani,
& my gifts from god – Lalithambigai & Perambigai

A tribute to the late Mr. Lee Kuan Yew –
20th century leader & 21st century teacher

Foreword

Leadership, both mystical and intricate by nature, has been studied for umpteen years. Over time, critical dimensions on this topic have been defined, modeled and elaborately discussed to improve one's leadership style and ability. From ages past to recent years, leaders have always been present. The only thing that has changed dramatically through the years is the application principles of leadership. Groundbreaking new research, coupled with newly found leadership strategies, have meant that the tactical application of leadership principles and methods are evolving and scaling new heights.

The topic on leadership, in particular administrative leadership, has always intrigued me. A complicated and vast topic, I elucidate administrative leadership using personal experiences, supporting it with relevant and practical situations as deemed appropriate. In this book, you will find citations and notable traits connected to qualities of successful and profound leaders. I have made conscious effort to acknowledge and reference ideas and quotes that are not originally mine. My humble apologies for any mistakes in referencing that may be contained in this book. If readers notice any such errors, I encourage you to please get in touch with me.

Consolidated with other highly regarded, pragmatic, and applicable theories, this book is a representation of my thought provoking ideas which render irrelevant the long drawn debate of whether leaders are born or made. A leader is one who possesses the ability to read, learn, and cultivate new knowledge and skills; and an interest in doing the same. This book has all the right ingredients thrown into it and is bursting with distinct flavors – a unique blend I would like to call my very own.

As leaders are omnipresent, I drew lessons from the people I saw, spoke with, and read about – especially administrative leaders I thought were incompetent and could do more in their position. I was consistently inspired by leaders from all around the world, co-workers and colleagues with leadership potential, and my own staff. Without a doubt, my most significant source of energy came from deep within. I take this opportunity to extend my greatest gratitude to all who have knowingly or unknowingly inspired me to write – Thank you.

Saravanan Sathiyaseelan

1. INTRODUCTION

There is arguably any single definition on leadership. Leadership is an abstract quality and has been difficult to either create or replicate. Leadership studies over the years have evolved[1][2], and reached a more balanced level of understanding in the 1990s.[3] Based on theories stemmed during the 20th century, many would argue that great leaders are born, not made.

Current studies have shown otherwise. Leadership traits do not change according to situations but rather, circumstances determine how each trait is applied. Intelligence, assertiveness, and at times, even physical attractiveness[4] are traits commonly connected to a leader. As leadership is too complex to be boiled down to a few key traits of an individual, it is widely assumed and accepted that a single trait or a set of traits does not make an extraordinary leader.

There is a very strong correlation between people who are energetic, assertive, determined, positive, inspiring, and diligent, and those who pursue their goals at any cost, work long hours, and strive for excellence. These individuals are able to display sound presentation and oratory abilities, behavioral flexibility, formulate solutions to difficult problems, work well under stress and deadlines, adapt to changing situations, and create well thought out plans for the future using intuitiveness and good judgment. As an example, reflect on the cognitive ability, change adaptation, and flexibility of Steve Jobs.

In my opinion, leaders are generally thought to possess the following qualities and behavioural traits - lead a team of people, inspire their followers, take charge of some kind of administration, wear many hats, be adept at communication and information management, perform specific tasks to achieve goals and objectives, and ensure people around them remain effective by knowing precisely what they need to do to remain effective. There may be more, but I shall limit the list for the purpose of this book.

Only a handful of great leaders encompass all of the traits listed above, but many have the ability to apply a number of them to succeed and function as front-runners and core leaders of their organization or country. Most managers do things right. But being a leader means you have to not only do things right, but do the right things. There are, of course, good and bad leaders.

As the topic on leadership is vast, I am going to focus on an important sub-field of leadership – administrative leadership. An administrative leader is one who makes sound decisions, leads in their course of work, is capable of largely influencing others to adopt their ideas, has the right mind-set and attitude, and is in charge of some kind of administration.

Since there is no single definition that is generally accepted by everyone, this book does not attempt to define leadership or explore deeply into existing leadership theories and traits. Instead, it tries to seek and surface the essence of a 21st century administrative leader. The tendency to focus on business leaders, social movement leaders, and political leaders is natural. However, administrative leaders are extraordinarily important figures as well. In most developed countries, administrative leaders manage between 20 to 30% of the workforce, and a quarter to half of the country's economy.[5]

Inequality has soared to an all-time high and large-scale resource shifts and relocation has increased competition for jobs and sustainable wages. There is dissatisfaction and people from all corners of the globe are desirous of change. The world needs administrative leaders who are bold and make changes swiftly, and yet know how to measure and deliver definite key outcomes without compromising employee motivation.

Leaders today need to take a step back and create opportunities in future to revisit problems commonly faced by leaders world-wide. Leaders nowadays are so obsessed about money and getting ahead that they have lost their humanity to a certain extent. They admire success so much that there is no room for others who do not want to chase the same dreams. It is unfortunate if you are reading this book and fall under this category.

In a chapter of this book ('Must-Have' Qualities), the qualities I believe constitute a worthy administrative leader are described. There is another chapter (8Cs') in which I define eight typical characteristics (or skills) of the 21st century administrative leader. The importance of embracing technology, the need to imagine and innovate, and make continuous improvements are some interesting concepts covered in another chapter of this book.

Another interesting chapter (rarely found in other leadership books) discusses the much debated topic of Diligence vs. Intelligence, and explores the possibility of changing leadership styles to suit your diligence and intelligence levels accordingly. This chapter is my personal favorite.

All chapters of this book are kept reasonably succinct. Anyone can read this book with ease within an acceptable time frame without getting bored, or losing focus and enthusiasm. Reading this book will open new avenues and possibilities for those who believe, and by shifting your paradigm on administrative leadership, hopefully enable you to learn new skills and create new opportunities!

2. POPULAR MYTHS

Administrative leadership, although largely analyzed and discussed, is one of the least understood concepts across all cultures and civilizations. Over the years, many scientists and researchers have emphasized the prevalence of this lack of understanding, stating that the existence of several flawed assumptions, or myths, concerning leadership often interferes with individuals' conception of what leadership is all about.[6][7]

2.1. *Myth No. 1 – Administrative Leadership is Attached to Position and Hierarchy*

Many consider leadership to be a trademark of a position or hierarchy in any organization or country. This can include formal roles being held by individuals - being the President, Chief Executive Officer, Head of Department/Division, Team Head/Leader, Superintendent, or Supervisor. The higher up your position on the corporate ladder, the more privileged you are deemed of adjudicating problems that may arise in the course of the work carried out at lower levels within the organization.

Simply put, based on your hierarchical position, you (the individual sitting at the top) are presumed to be an expert in adjudicating problems. It is this bureaucratic structure that forms the basis for the appointment of heads or chiefs of administrative subdivisions in the organization, and endows them with the authority attached to their position.[8]

Contrary of this belief, anyone can be a leader at any level. After all, leadership is the ability to influence people. You can be in an informal role and still influence a colleague or co-worker. Leaders are recognized by their capacity for caring for others, clear communication, and a commitment to persist.[9]

Authority to enforce, command and govern is granted to an individual in a managerial position under the assumption that this person is responsible, capable, competent and in possession of adequate personal attributes to match his/her position accordingly to the hierarchy and authority endowed to them. If personal attributes and competence are proven to be deficient, anyone may choose to challenge and confront this individual's given authority, and reduce them to that of a mere figurehead.

With great position and power comes greater responsibility and challenges. The higher up you are on the corporate ladder by virtue of your position, the more things you are expected to be in charge and prove. However, administrative leadership is one particular area in which everyone bears equal responsibility.

Formulating goals and objectives is a shared responsibility and should not be left to a group of people or an individual sitting at the top of an organization (or country) to handle. When everyone has a sense of belonging, the vision and mission of the organization becomes a common and shared target. Excellent administrative leaders deliberately empower those below them so that everyone is able to strive for the organization's goals and objectives. In a very indirect manner, everyone becomes an administrative leader through such empowerment.

2.2. *Myth No. 2 – Only Administrative Leaders Make Decisions*

Organizations, regardless of size and culture, comprise people who make decisions daily. Decision making is regarded as merely a problem solving activity, although the process is much more complicated. A large portion of recent studies have revealed how the human brain functions when making rational and irrational decisions. Some have even argued that most decisions are made unconsciously.[10]

Though there are still several unknowns in the science of decision making, the fact remains that as human beings, we have a natural ability to make decisions regardless of positions held. We make decisions daily – what to eat, what to drink, where to shop, which route to take to work, when to rest, when to visit the washroom, etcetera. The list goes on.

You need not be in a leadership position to make a critical decision. The only distinct difference, perhaps, could lie in the responsibility one has to take on when a decision goes wrong. That remains a virtue pegged to an individual's position within the organization.

For instance, let us examine the case of a front desk customer service officer supporting operations in a student services centre. The job of a customer service officer seems straight forward. They make countless crucial decisions on a daily basis – how to comfort a student in distress, choosing right words to calm an angry parent, when to place an order for paper, how to react to difficult customers, where to search for inquiries, and so on.

These may not be key persons and their decisions may not carry huge implications, but still the decisions made are essential. If only key personnel in managerial posts are to handle these matters, daily haggling and quibbling in the student services centre would become an inevitable norm. Anywhere and at any time, a team fully equipped with capable decision makers will be very efficient and administratively superior.

In other words, I would say an unparalleled skill like decision making is not limited only to administrative leaders. Anyone within the organization is capable of standing out prominently when it comes to decision making. Decision making is a vital skill not just for leaders, but for human beings in general.

Personally speaking, I believe we all go through critical phases in life where our decision making skills and abilities get tested. We actually make many major decisions just to achieve the basic things in life – purchasing an efficient car, buying an affordable home, choosing your field in education, and deciding when to get married and how many children to have. So, if you ever think that you are not capable of making decisions at your workplace, think again!

2.3. <u>Myth No. 3 – Administrative Leaders Only Need to Mingle with the 'Higher Ups'</u>

If you say that you are a leader at any level within your organization, my first question to you will be, "Do you know the name of all your workers beneath you, including your cleaners and drivers?" Although this may sound strange, it apparently makes perfect sense when you think deeper. The job of a leader is to get things done - achieve key performance indicators, meet objectives, and produce favourable outcomes.

Having said this, how would one relate to a cleaner and interact with that individual to get a simple task completed without knowing their name? For an able administrative leader, no one in the organization should be a liability - not contributing nor adding value to the company's growth and profit margins.

Pause and think for a moment, wouldn't it be good to establish a close and positive relationship with your driver? After all, you spend much time traveling. Usually, people tend to treat and react to you the same way you do to others. So establishing more personal contact with your driver (by being more interactive and engaging), would transform your daily journey into a more cheerful one and directly contribute to you functioning more effectively at work – your mood affects your work productivity every day.

The cleaners with whom you interact almost daily but do not know personally are in actual fact an asset and should be well treated as they can indirectly contribute to your organization. As an administrative leader, you should make it a point to mingle with all workers at all levels if you want to achieve positive results in all aspects.

Based on a preliminary study conducted by the European Agency for Safety and Health at Work, there are strong evidences indicating that the high overall quality of a working environment, including good housekeeping, is essential for improving productivity.[11] Since there is strong correlation that links a good working environment to productivity, it is in the best interest of a good and effective administrative leader to have a better understanding of the positive effects that a good working environment brings about. This understanding also is crucial for relevant policies to support the implementation of effective health and safety governance for the organization.

You must have often heard of workers lower down in the command chain complaining about those higher up. In reality, the lesser the distance between you as a leader and the workers underneath you, the closer you can actually get to achieving positive results. With such an attitude, a good administrative leader will be able to achieve a win-win situation by getting the support of those reporting directly to you and beyond. Getting support from and earning the respect of those around you is impressive. Getting everyone in the organization to perform a desired job to your advantage is both admirable and enviable.

Thus, I would say an effective administrative leader needs to mingle with not only the superiors, but also with others who may indirectly be able to contribute to the organization and its profit margins. As a leader, every opportunity you get to bridge a gap between the individuals you come in close contact with is an added advantage and privilege.

An engaging leader of the 21st century needs to comprehend the feelings and other external parameters that could indirectly affect the intrinsic motivational levels of those around if (s)he is to meet the primary focus of his/her job – getting things done!

2.4. *Myth No. 4 – Administrative Leaders are Highly Qualified*

Both business and political landscapes tend to only accept leaders who are academically qualified. This is a common practice in many places, but a worrying trend indeed. A leader is too often stereotyped to be someone who has attained high academic qualifications. More recently, this has been widely debated and has oftentimes raised many eyebrows.

Bill Gates, founder of Microsoft, is known to be one of the world's richest men and Harvard's most successful dropout in its history. When Gates dropped out of Harvard, he talked his decision over with his parents, who agreed after seeing the burning passion for and commitment to starting up his own company.

Alongside Gates stands another famous name - India's current Prime Minister, Narendra Damodardas Modi. Modi has been described by his teachers to be an average student in his early days. As a child, he helped his father sell tea at the Vadnagar railway station. He later ran a tea stall with his brother near a bus terminus.[12]

What do you see common in the two examples above? The most notable commonality would be the decision to pursue their passion and dreams larger than life - they didn't reach their current positions due to academic qualifications. Many more belong to this category, but I am unable to list them all. In making this point, I am in no way arguing that academic qualifications are unimportant. I am, however, questioning the significance of its relevance to and impact on the attainment of success.

If you are a soccer fan like I am, take a good look at the World Cup held once every four years. Many skillful and talented players come and go, and history has their names written on it. They are very popular everywhere they go. Yet more often than not, the teams comprised of several skillful players do not win the World Cup. The team that plays together tastes victory. This is no coincidence.

Applying the same theory, a team of highly qualified scholars cannot run an organization or country well on their own. Teamwork is more important than both skills and knowledge combined. A single tree cannot become a forest; success and victory cannot be a result of just having administrative leaders who come with high qualifications alone!

Each of us should attempt to learn continuously throughout our lifetime. As an advocate of continuous learning, I personally read a lot to increase my knowledge, watch educational programmes that increase my exposure, and embark on short courses each year to develop my skills – the attitude one has towards cultivating new skills and knowledge at any given point of their life is more important than academic qualifications alone. There are ample opportunities out there to be seized for those who seek them.

Academic qualifications are important and play a certain role in shaping one's success, but they do not determine the heights to which an individual can soar. I often say to others that academic qualifications can get you an interview, but it will not necessarily get you through the interview successfully.

3. From Manual to Automation – Technology is here to stay!

What is so iconic about organizations like Microsoft, Apple, Google and Amazon? At a glance, it is not their logo or fanciful marketing taglines that strike a chord in our minds. These reputable brands are anchored and strongly driven by technology.

With the advancement of technology, the world has changed drastically. Technology has advanced and caused the world to shrink so swiftly that we are now able to communicate all around the world without needing to travel.

It is amazing how an organization can strategically position itself at the forefront, ahead of its rivals by harnessing latest technology. Through the application of right methodologies and appropriate technology, a company is capable of achieving remarkable growth in a short span of time.

In any strategic master plan of an organization, there will typically be an expansion plan which would depend on harnessing technology to the fullest of its potential. Organizations nowadays know the kind of impact technology can make, and the edge it provides over immediate rivals and competitors.

Social networking has impacted the business world so deeply that it has transformed the way information is obtained. According to Gartner, an IT research and advisory company, about 60% of Fortune 1000 companies used social media in some form or another to improve customer relations in 2010.

Now, with social media and networks such as Facebook, Twitter, and other online forums having stirred a revolution, a significant 92% of leading marketers agree that they use these platforms extensively for their companies, regardless of organization size.[13]

Social media and networks have become a norm for organizations seeking sustenance, expansion, and a leading edge over other market leaders. These platforms, when utilized correctly, should be able to provide uplift to an organization and an improvement in company positioning.

Similarly, even teaching methodologies have shifted away from conventional methods and now incorporate technology usage extensively. iPads, iPods, and iPhones are now commonly owned by teenagers and young adults. From gaming apps to scientific learning apps, everything is readily available and accessible. There is an overwhelming amount of information out there and with technology, such information is now easily and instantly attainable.

Students use various educational apps and note-taking materials to construct their learning. Such apps have conquered a position in mainstream education. Teachers embrace 21st century pedagogical skills by giving students easy access to learning materials anytime and anywhere, thus empowering them to conduct self-directed learning.

As mentioned earlier, technology, when applied appropriately, can and will benefit everyone depending on it. In short, technology is being embraced to engage and empower individuals all over the globe. For instance, schools in Singapore use a wide array of multimedia technology for instructional purposes – both National University of Singapore (NUS) and Nanyang Technological University (NTU) medical schools commenced iPad apps not too long ago.

If a vast majority of people – from a 3 year-old child to an 80 year-old elderly can be immersed in the use of iPads and the latest smartphones, why should it not be used with students to enhance their learning? An online-mediated teaching like e-learning becomes a part of mainstream curriculum, where textbooks and traditional lectures are replaced with mobile technology.

This intervention has been found to boost creativity and encourage adaptability to responses for 21st century learners. Knowing the importance and understanding the fundamental nature of technology and its centrality in education, leading universities are jumping on the bandwagon to capitalise on this fast moving trend.

In support of going green, organizations worldwide are now adopting 'paperless' policies. Companies achieve their 'paperless' goals and ambitions by harnessing the aid of technology. As organizations worldwide aim to maximize productivity and reduce waste in order to promote a healthier and happier world, technology comes in useful to achieve green initiatives.

With amazing technological discoveries, boundaries are constantly challenged and limits stretched. As management and information systems, technology, and social media and networks are critical in paving the way for innovative breakthroughs, reaching out to people, multiplying positive effects, and refinement of business processes (particularly as compared to merely improvising using existing resources), it is vital that an effective and efficient administrative leader stays abreast and if possible ahead of the latest trend-setting technological transformations.

In today's environment, the use of information technology and various other technologies are important enablers in learning, teaching, research, sharing and administration. An organization striving to make an impact on a global scale should leverage information technology to multiply their outreach efforts, and drive user-friendly integrated administration processes that improve business efficiencies.

As part of administrative excellence, leaders of Small and Medium Enterprises (SMEs) and Multi-National Corporations (MNCs) should always create timely opportunities to holistically re-examine various systems and processes across the organization. I.T. is an important pillar in any organization and should be kept alive and healthy by the administrative leader to spur innovation and attain greater synergy.

The impetus for such transformations, trivial or otherwise, is usually external rather than internal, and is typically regarded as a necessary evil. The leader who refuses to embrace change brought about by rapid advancement and expansion of technological developments risks becoming outdated and obsolete. Technology is a gift; the ability to embrace and use this gift wisely is wisdom.

4. 'Must-Have' Qualities

4.1. *Attitude*

Just like a little light overcomes total darkness, a little positivity in your attitude is all it takes to overcome complete negativity. As an administrative leader, your attitude is under constant scrutiny. Your followers are closely observing your actions (it is important to them as a guide). Your mind-set and positive attitudes are being closely monitored everywhere and at all times – how you deal with problems, what goals to set, why changes are made, and even the style of your presentation and communication.

In life, there is a solution to every problem. Having a problem is common, as no one in this world can honestly declare that they live a life fully contented without any problems. However, how you view and approach problems is a totally different ball game. Having a problem is like holding a small marble using two fingers – if you keep it close to your eyes, the marble is all you can see; but if you bring it further away from the eye, the marble appears small and you can see more apart from the marble. So, keep the marble (problem) far so that it does not limit or obstruct your vision.

It is your attitude that matters, for in any organization or country, the leader's attitude helps determine the attitudes of his/her followers. Your attitude and reactions to chaotic and crisis situations help shape your reliability as a leader, and more importantly, earns you your credibility and showcases you as a respectable person or otherwise. Your attitude towards problems and the way in which you deal with them is often used as an example for your co-workers, colleagues, and subordinates to follow.

I opine that an administrative leader has one of two common types of attitudes when it comes to handling difficult situations - Fight or Flight! The first attitude is that of administrative leaders whom we need. In times of problems and turmoil, good administrative leaders effectively solve problems because they have the right attitude. They realize that problems are a norm and an inevitable part of life.

They see problems as an opportunity to turn things around and set things right. They fully understand that a problem is only a problem and not trouble unless they take a wrong decision to the issue at hand. They are swift to act, react, and proactively put in safety nets and contingencies with the right action plans.

If there is trouble, they are also the first ones to step up to the meaningful task of accepting blame and driving a culture of moving forward by not lingering on the past. At the same time, these leaders also work out the right action plans and mitigate risks involved as much as possible, taking experiential learning into their own hands and not leaving the future of the company or country at stake - they maintain a positive attitude, think about new opportunities for tomorrow, and do not focus on the past problems.

As for the second attitude of flight, this attitude is commonly linked to administrative leaders we do not need and can do without. In times of difficulty, they will most likely flee the scene and leave others stranded; regardless of whether they are to be blamed or not. This group of administrative leaders hold the marble (problem) so close to their eyes that they are oblivious and effectively blind to the many other opportunities and possible avenues. They are short-sighted and do not make attempts to use such opportunities to set things right. They often resort to isolation and silence, thinking that in so doing, problems will resolve themselves or just go away.

The administrative leader's vision and goals should remain unaltered, with plans and goals focused more on the long term rather than short. It is important to support your leadership qualities with a good and positive attitude despite your leadership style as different styles suit different organizations and all can be successful in their own right.

When making goals, be realistic, positive, flexible (to a certain extent), and take a consultative approach to ensure your staff feel comfortable. They should feel that your goals for them are reasonable and achievable. Your subordinates and co-workers should not feel pressured to achieve your goals and as you lead them with the correct attitude, they too will learn to see things in a positive light. You don't just work towards your goals as an individual, but encourage everyone to cohesively achieve your goals as a team.

The best administrative leaders inspire their teams to work smart and not just work hard. They inspire them and teach them to view things positively (even challenges) and reward them for reaching goals and performing well. Rewards can come in numerous forms, but the best I know comes from sincere recognition and acknowledgment.

Sometimes, although not always, you can choose to reward each staff in a manner that is more personal and meaningful to them. For instance, some prefer flexibility in working hours, while some others may choose a good training/grooming session instead. No matter what, reward each individual for their contributions by the book (HR policies) and based on the authority that has been endowed to you.

Administrative leadership today is more exciting than ever when you have the right attitude. Our attitude is one of our most valuable assets. Our attitudes determine what we see, how we handle our feelings, words we choose to speak, and how we act. Life's challenges do not concern themselves with who the smarter, stronger, or faster person is; eventually, the individual who has the right mind-set and a positive attitude will be the one who overcomes such challenges and makes further accomplishments.

4.2. *Self-discipline*

"Self-discipline begins with the mastery of your thoughts. If you don't control what you think, you can't control what you

do. Simply, self-discipline enables you to think first and act forward."

Napoleon Hill (Author, quote taken from Napoleon Hill quotes – Brainy Quotes)

Self-discipline is a very special quality that allows a person to stand out and be unique. A capable administrative leader should possess self-discipline at all times. It is a constant challenge to maintain self-discipline as there is much temptation all around. To make matters worse, the world is globalized in many aspects and organizations (even countries) want to get ahead of the stiff competition at any cost.

As an example, assume that you plan to participate in an upcoming marathon and you are serious about completing your very first marathon by end of the year. First and foremost, you have an objective – one that is clear, specific, and measurable. The next step will be to prepare yourself both mentally and physically to run a marathon.

If you ever ran a marathon, you will know the importance of doing long runs and clocking high mileage. But it is not easy – training is time consuming and takes serious commitment. You need to dedicate plenty of time to train and rest well in order to be mentally and physically ready for such a challenge.

This is where your self-discipline comes in. You should draft a training schedule that suits your work schedule and does not compromise family time. Next comes the harder part – actually following your training regime. Most of us find it easy to reach the first stage of drafting a schedule, but never clear the hurdle of following through with the said schedule. This action requires self-discipline.

The same principles apply in a corporate setting. For instance, you are tasked to lead a sales team and your top management has given you clear directives on your KPIs. To achieve your sales target, you must first have an objective – one that is clear, specific, and measurable. The next step is to prepare your team both mentally and physically to achieve this target.

You should brief your team of your expectations (and targets), draft a schedule for adherence, set KPIs for each individual, and inspire them to achieve their goals. Self-discipline is needed for you to stay focused to achieve your key objectives and also at the same time to keep your team actively engaged throughout the assignments. Self-discipline is believed to aid in the creation of new habits of thought and action aimed at improving yourself and reaching goals.

Self-discipline helps you to control your tasks and activities. By controlling your tasks and activities, you become more constructive and productive. So when you set a schedule and make it a point to stick closely to it, you get what you want eventually. Furthermore, when your colleagues, co-workers and subordinates see you as a person of routine and self-discipline, they follow suit. This is also another way of setting trends and practices for others to follow.

In the area of personal integrity, more than before, the time has come for administrative leaders to exercise self-discipline. We have read and heard news of numerous scandals, cases when contracts and deals have gone wrong due to personal greed, and of incidents in which details of confidential dealings have been leaked in return for other trade-offs.

Rules may be in place but there are just as many areas that remain unclearly defined, more commonly in the business world where profit matters. When there are too many ambiguous areas, some administrative leaders give in to temptations and tend to abuse policies by testing loopholes for their own profit and personal gain. They skew towards practices that benefit only them, become biased and manipulative, and trade their humanity for monetary and other personal benefits.

Self-discipline begins in one's mind, so no one has an excuse to shy away from this quality. Self-discipline helps you in two major ways - to develop habits that help you achieve your goals/targets and to stay firm on the path of righteousness. I have been with leaders who show their true nature (ill-disciplined behaviour) when it comes to appraisal and promotion exercises.

They become very biased (reasons could be many but none worthy of specific mention), and follow their 'own protocol' and not that of the company. Favouritism is still very prevalent in many administrative leaders who comb through their own personal favourites to be promoted, with disregard for the person(s) who are truly deserving of promotion. Nothing could disgust followers more, yet unfortunately, leaders driven by their own selfish nature still have to be tolerated.

When self-discipline is no longer critical for leadership, objectives, rules and humanity all take a drastic hit. The effects are detrimental and adverse, and they very possibly leave no benefits to be reaped. Self-discipline should not be compromised at all costs. When self-discipline is left unguarded, standards and values of good administrative leadership erode very quickly. Mistakes are magnified, reputations damaged, profits diminished, and social and economic status roiled.

4.3. *Knowledge*

You walk into a car showroom. You may know some basics about cars and have a certain expectation of the type of car you are looking to purchase. However, you would still have many burning questions within you that you seek answers to – what is the petrol consumption, how often will you need to perform an oil change, what is the car's engine power and torque, laden weight, engine capacity, and probably a number of other essential questions that may persuade you to make the decision to purchase.

You spot a salesperson who walks over to you after acknowledging your presence. With no time wasted, you begin to ask all the essential questions mentioned above. The salesperson evades some of your questions and provides very vague answers to many others. He appears unsure of his company products. In this scenario, would you continue to make the purchase?

My guess is – NO. If your answer is no as well, you have just joined thousands, if not millions, of others on this planet who feel that knowledge is POWER! Whatever business you do, whether small or big, you need knowledge of your business. Knowledge is not limited only to the sales or marketing departments, but to everyone right from the top to the bottom.

The only difference is the specific areas you are knowledgeable about. The power of knowledge is never to be underestimated.

Each individual is gauged by the knowledge (s)he has on his/her work areas. This is commonly termed specific domain knowledge. Having said this, one might wonder, an administrative leader like a CEO of a large organization could have a gargantuan problem at hand as (s)he has such a mammoth task in overseeing several departments under him/her. Many argue that it is simply impossible to have knowledge of everything that is happening in all parts of an organization. I hate to say this, but I wholeheartedly agree.

The larger your organization is, the harder it is to gain an insight into every single detail that is happening around you. But the good news is, knowledge can be cultivated and improved by listening and talking to others. More importantly, things continue to change. Top leaders of large corporate companies keep themselves abreast of all relevant news and events by being resourceful.

As an administrative leader, the most important news to you should be those that can affect your company's reputation, profits, customers, and staff morale. To be efficient and effective, a capable administrative leader must decide what to take in and when to do so, maintain reliable and informative resources in areas that really matter, and keep an open mind towards learning and develop a healthy appetite for the same.

Remember, you can only make critical decisions to prevent your company from collapsing, or decide when to launch that new product of yours when you simultaneously have knowledge, know how to apply that knowledge, and act on it. Knowledge alone without action is also useless to a certain extent.

Relating back to the example of the car salesperson, he could not have won over the potential client simply by having sufficient knowledge of his company's products. Answering all queries does not necessarily mean that a sale will be confirmed. The only way for the salesman to accomplish his target and secure a sale is by using his product knowledge properly and channelling his energy into convincing the potential customer to purchase a car that would best fit their needs and expectations. Therefore, knowledge application is equally important as the knowledge itself.

Knowledge of your specific domain, when applied with conviction, dedication, and passion, can bring you to the next level of your career. On the other hand, lack of knowledge can be extremely detrimental to your company and eventually you, together with the company, will face the danger of losing competitive advantage in your business.

Every market leader portrays a distinct difference and unique advantage they have in order to gain a competitive advantage over other industry players. This brings me to my next point – knowledge of other industry players and their products is equally important as having adequate knowledge of your own product.

Imagine that your company is new to the education industry and is planning to launch a new degree programme. You start from scratch with a long term vision, mission, implementation and execution plans. Rationally speaking, you need more than vision, mission, implementation and execution plans – you need to know how to make your new programme as unique as possible to stand out among competitors and grow amidst an already dense market.

For that, you need extensive knowledge of your competitors - what they already offer, how not to duplicate what is already being offered, the benchmark for the type of programme you are intending to deliver, and methods that can be employed to attract a different and more diverse target audience in order to stay ahead of the competition.

Knowledge is grossly underestimated by many around the world. The simple and hard truth is that knowledge is indeed power. To sum up what has been covered, I will use a pyramid (I call this the Knowledge Pyramid) to illustrate the various types of knowledge an administrative leader needs to stay ahead.

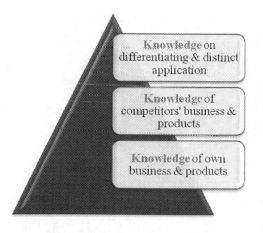

Figure 1: Knowledge Pyramid

"Knowledge of own business & products" is found at the base of the pyramid since this is the main basis through which your company is founded. "Knowledge of competitors' business & products" is crucial and also the key factor that could either 'make' or 'break' your own business as this helps you to focus on differentiating your own products to ensure your strategies can be modified and not duplicated. At the apex of the pyramid is "Knowledge on differentiating & distinct application". With knowledge of your own product and that of your competitors, you are now able to do something different to ensure product/business needs are to your advantage, focusing on application principles that are uniquely tailored to meet the changing needs of the market. This is the rationale for the Knowledge Pyramid to be designed in the current manner.

4.4. *Humility*

Humility, an act of lowering yourself to the level of others or treating everybody as equal, is a strong quality that enables an individual to behave with no disparity of any sort towards others. In life, we determine what happens to us by controlling circumstances that happen around us (at least most of us try to do this). Our actions reap consequences that follow.

As an administrative leader, you would prefer to hold your head up high and walk with pride. Of course, there is no wrong in that as you may have worked hard and earned yourself the recognition to reach this status. However, if you always walk looking up, you might trip and fall. There is a saying, "the higher you are, the harder you fall".

In a similar context, the more time you spend looking up high, the more the chances of you falling. You may be surprised that it only takes a small stone to make you trip. So, you should first agree that it is important to occasionally look down; not on others but to acknowledge the presence of those around you.

Have you attended meetings where the boss or a department head replied to a typical question thrown at him/her by saying, "let me check with my staff and get back to you"? What does this imply? To me, it simply proves that this boss is only a spokesperson by virtue of position and not by virtue of knowledge. In other words, this person is not the SME (Subject Matter Expert).

I can guess the likely thoughts running through most of your minds right now: why should the boss know everything? That is true, and I agree. Hold that thought and I'll clarify in a bit. But just before I elaborate and explain, let me share with you a personal experience that remains close to my heart to this day.

It happened during one of my meetings with many other department heads (the stakeholders, you can say). The agenda of the meeting was to simply provide an update to all the stakeholders and gather the concurrence of the project steering committee. Basically, a number of major decisions had to be made on resource and space optimization, budget matters, process redesigning, and project ownership. These truly indispensable concerns were slowing the progress of the entire project. So this meeting was aimed at addressing all these issues.

As I was championing the project, it was my responsibility to conduct the presentation. After I presented, I realized no one had any questions or clarifications. Quite puzzled by the absence in questions despite the magnitude of issues pending a decision, I reiterated and emphasized that we needed to make these decisions promptly so that the project could proceed on schedule (those present for this meeting were holding senior appointments and therefore, I thought it would be easy for them to make these decisions).

I was astounded when a number of them replied that they needed to check with the SMEs on such matters. Initially, I was agitated by their irresponsible replies. I had clearly indicated in my email to them the importance of this meeting (decisions needed to be made) and suggested for them to bring along all significant people capable of contributing and making constructive decisions.

So, annoyed and yet curious, I asked why the SMEs were not present. The senior appointment holders simply answered that the SMEs were not needed because of their (relatively lower) position in the organizational hierarchy (experts in certain areas are not always sitting on top). On hearing such reasoning, I was no longer annoyed nor agitated, but simply dumbfounded. I felt sympathetic towards them for their petty mind-sets. The bottom line is this: these administrative leaders needed a paradigm shift - to discard their old schools of thought about leadership, hierarchy, decision making, and significant contributions!

Connecting this to what I had highlighted earlier, leaders need not know everything but they need to know enough at least to make decisions. For that, they need to practise humility and accept the fact that employees at all levels can be involved in the decision making process.

In this case, the leaders were not humble enough to consult SMEs below their level, nor were they considerate enough to engage in a productive meeting. They should have read my email clearly and come prepared to make decisions. The absence of humility led to their belief that the working group (who are the embodiment of knowledge) could be conveniently omitted.

They excluded the SMEs from the meeting as they judged themselves to be superior. The absence of humility was obvious and notable in their leadership styles and beliefs. The meeting eventually concluded with no objectives met, and I had to organize another. Just a gentle reminder at this juncture – meetings are important and, as much as possible, face to face meetings should conclude with constructive decisions made. Time and effort taken to arrange and attend meetings should not go wasted.

Have you seen truly great administrative leaders who have, in their lifetime, performed miracles - people deemed unqualified to be CEOs but who remained in their positions for decades, were able to turnaround a company from debts to profits in little time, outperformed their rivals and made their companies reap huge profits (good enough to make it to the Fortune 500), and who transformed never-before heard names to buzzwords spoken by all? One such example of a CEO who turned a company from debts to profits in little time is Joseph Sullivan. You can look up on the internet to read more about Joseph Sullivan and how he turned the fate of his company around.

Such leaders exist but they truly do not believe in flashing fashionable personal belongings and living in luxury. A humble administrative leader with extreme will and perseverance can overcome the odds and succeed against other competitors in the business because humility is acknowledged, recognized and well accepted by all followers. Respect begets respect.

4.5. *Integrity*

A key ingredient to administrative leadership is integrity.

"Let me define a leader. He must have vision and passion and not be afraid of any problem. Instead, he should know how to defeat it. Most importantly, he must work with integrity."

A. P. J. Abdul Kalam *(Indian scientist, 11th President of India from 2002 to 2007, quote taken from A. P. J. Abdul Kalam quotes – Brainy Quotes)*

Why so - because the thoughts and actions of administrative leaders cascade down and influence the way others think and act around this person (in an organization or country). The higher your level of integrity is, the more confidence people place in you. Therefore, the easier your followers view your behaviours as acceptable norms to closely follow suit.

The topic of integrity has been up for debate since the start of leadership. One thing for sure: integrity is a defining characteristic for anyone claiming to be a leader. There is no need for discussion of the importance of leaders possessing integrity as an essential quality because it is commonly known and widely accepted. Instead, I would like to talk about how leaders with integrity are widely accepted by their colleagues and function better in their roles as a result.

Integrity is about consistently walking the talk and doing the right thing, at all times without succumbing to greed and temptations, whether or not you are being watched. Exceptional individuals who have demonstrated integrity (being truthful, trustworthy, principled, honest, and not deceptive) are readily accepted as leaders by many. An administrative leader possessing traits closely related to integrity will be well liked by co-workers, superiors, and subordinates. What exactly is integrity to your followers?

Administrative leaders who have proven their integrity and earned respect amongst their peers are thought to be competent and adaptable; competent in the use of diplomatic measures to solve problems, and adaptable to the changing demands of the environment or situation at hand. These particular individuals are viewed as honest leaders to whom these followers could turn when there are issues to settle or even for a friendly chat outside of work.

Once you have proven your mettle and earned your place as a leader with integrity, you automatically break boundaries that exist between you (the leader) and your staff (the followers). Your co-workers, colleagues and staff will begin to treat you as a friend, let you in on their personal conversations, and soon, even into their private lives and inner secrets.

When you are seen as a friend, it is easier to get things moving and completed on time. Moreover, as a leader who has become a trustworthy friend, you now have the advantage of understanding their fears, uncertainties, weaknesses, vulnerabilities, and deep rooted thoughts. With some caution (without crossing professional boundaries), you now can address the root problems that may affect their work outcomes and performances. This way, objectives are met more amicably and quickly.

But, be aware! When you start moving into their personal space, you are exposing yourself to some risks as well. The 'black and white' areas defined between superiors and subordinates now turn 'grey'. If you are unable to practice strict discipline and professionalism when called for, you may risk getting drawn into their personal problems. This, therefore, is a double-edged sword!

"Integrity is the essence of everything successful."

Richard Buckminster Fuller (American Inventor, quote taken from Richard Buckminster Fuller quotes - Brainy Quotes)

Integrity is not something that you can clearly showcase to others as it is more often felt than noticed. With integrity, you can overcome even the toughest problems as it will help to pull all necessary resources in your favor when you need them. Without integrity, even the slightest problems you might encounter can blow out of proportion and limit your progress and profits.

All leaders are expected to govern with integrity. If you feel devoid of integrity, I can share with you some simple tips to increase your level of integrity (note that I say simple, not easy). First, put aside your personal interests and gains. If you have a number of decisions to make, take the decision that best benefits others. Basically, be more selfless in your thoughts and actions, and serve everyone to your best ability.

Next, keep your moral conduct upright. The world wants to see administrative leaders as people who behave consistently no matter what the situation may be. So, no matter what life throws at you, you as a leader, are expected to do the right thing for the right reason regardless of circumstances.

Integrity is one of the top attributes of a great leader. Administrative leaders with integrity place their followers on top of their priority list. Over the past decade or so, the large number of scandals involving top echelon leaders have been making waves in the media. These waves are not getting smaller over time, but need to come to a halt as they constantly challenge the concept of integrity in leaders. Living the way of righteousness, regardless of the consequence, is the hallmark of integrity.

4.6. *Motivation*

As an administrative leader, your duty is primarily to produce desirable results and attain success for your organization (or country). The difficult task lies not in changing employees' behaviour but in giving them a reason to change their behavioural norms and patterns, with an understanding of the specific gains and benefits such change will bring about for each individual.

Sound administrative leaders know that every human has needs, expectations, and independent motivational levels. Staying motivated with a sense of purpose and belonging, having direction for achieving your goal and being able to stay on course to keep everyone around you motivated, is more easily achieved when you are passionate about what you do.

Motivation is a powerful afterburner that can propel anyone to soar to great heights of success. Motivation helps foster innovative thinking and creative solutions that provide you the courage to keep all around you motivated without the need to be compelled. To add on, motivation drives you to take action on your plans.

When you have great clarity on your action plans and a very vivid end state of your goals, self-confidence automatically builds up, boosting the confidence of those around you. Self-confident individuals do not doubt themselves, their abilities, and decisions they make. As a bonus, such individuals also have the ability to project this self-confidence onto others building trust on their mission and gaining commitment to achieve the unimaginable.

Employee motivation can be described as the willingness to exert high levels of effort towards defined goals, conditioned by the effort's ability to satisfy some individual needs. For employees to be motivated, the administrative leader must first be able to identify their needs. There are a number of theories on motivation – the most well-known is Maslow's Hierarchy of Needs.

Maslow's Hierarchy of Needs distinguishes the five levels of needs of any human being. They are categorized according to a hierarchy. It starts off with physiological needs like hunger, thirst, sleep, and sex. The second in rank is given to safety, which includes security and protection from physical and emotional harm. Coming in third is social needs. This basically encompasses affection, a sense of belonging, and acceptance. Next in place is esteem. Esteem covers self-respect, autonomy, achievement, status, recognition and attention. Self-actualization falls in at the top of the pyramid comprising growth, potential realization and self-fulfilment.

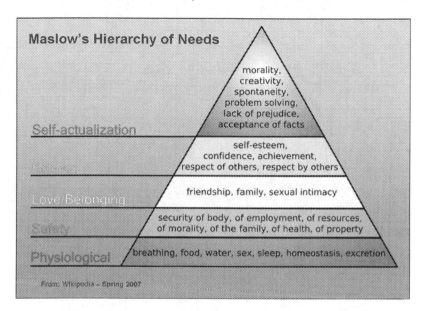

Figure 2: Maslow's Hierarchy of Needs
(from Wikipedia, spring 2007)

Strictly speaking, some form of motivation is necessary for anyone to work hard towards achieving the organizational goals. As far as a country is concerned, the citizens are her greatest and most valuable asset. The same applies to an organization. The growth and development of people may be one of the highest callings of administrative leadership. Administrative leaders who continue to grow personally and bring growth to their organization, and in a larger context, to their country, will influence and impact the lives of many and develop a highly motivated team.

A very common but grave error an administrative leader can commit is to pass negative remarks and criticism. Criticism or condemnation in any form does not do any good to anyone. As a traditional saying goes, when we point a finger at someone, the other four fingers are pointed back at ourselves. You must be very careful not to point a finger at your colleague or subordinate and have four other fingers pointed back at you.

The effects of criticisms can be clearly observed in a classroom. Students often excelling in their academic performance are those who are highly motivated. Motivation is one key factor that pumps more than mere adrenaline into your bloodstream. Criticism, on the other hand, is the best exterminator of motivation. When a student loses the motivation to study due to criticism, there is an automatic decline in the academic performance of that student. This does not necessarily mean that the student is no longer fit for study, but simply means that the child has lost interest in studying.

No one is perfect in this world. This is the universal law that remains steady and unaffected by time. However, we make a bigger mistake by failing to understand the laws of nature. It is good to learn that everyone errs and we are only humans. By forgiving, we become capable administrative leaders and even much better human beings.

In the topic of motivation, much has been said about motivating your followers, but never overlook or be ignorant of the fact that you too need to stay motivated. For most people, motivating oneself poses a greater challenge than motivating others. History is filled with great leaders who dreamt big and had great plans but never achieved their goals as they lacked the courage and desire to succeed.

Staying motivated, or self-motivating, is similar to filling your car with the top grade fuel. All cars run on fuel but for some, the quality of the fuel matters – this differentiates the true leaders from the mediocre, the 'great' from the 'good'. Never settle for anything less when you can get more. As an administrative leader, you should never be satisfied with the status quo. You must have in you the overwhelming desire for constant change that promotes improvement.

When you have the burning desire to attain success, motivation is the key that gives you the reason to act. To stay motivated, you must have a meaningful and valid goal, and with the right amount of desire, you will achieve excellence. After all, like the saying goes, you are what you think and you will be tested and measured up against how you convert your thoughts into actions. The ordinary administrative leader is concerned about consistently motivating others. The extraordinary administrative leader is passionate about staying motivated to motivate others!

5. 8 Cs'

5.1. _Credibility_

In the world of leadership, credibility is everything. How would you judge a manager of an insurance agency divulging confidential information of clients, or an educator of an educational institution revealing personal information of students? It is a clear breach of trust. As an administrative leader, you are regarded as a symbol of trust. When your actions show that you are not worthy of trust, you risk losing your credibility.

Credibility is not limited to mere trust, but much more. When you hear a presentation, you would rather it be presented by a credible source as compared to someone you consider to be a novice (or not as credible). Similarly, a credible salesman would be able to achieve sales targets more easily as compared to someone who is unable to adequately prove their credibility.

Credibility may be enhanced by a person's oratory abilities, but is definitely not established by that ability alone. When you are backed by strong credibility, it acts as a testament to your capability and capacity for functioning as a leader in your own field or area. People are willing to work and do things for credible administrative leaders as it is easier to believe that these leaders will far exceed others when it comes to achieving targets and goals. Credibility, in a way, further enhances your image to function as a capable and convincing administrative leader.

Credibility is never earned overnight. It takes patience, dedication, diligence, and consistency to establish. Gaining trust is more than getting your followers to listen to you. It is, in fact, doing the right things for the right reasons even when you know there is no one watching. You must be true to your actions, seen to be transparent in your dealings, and free of any ulterior motives.

The first hurdle that stands between you and your credibility is your knowledge. If you are knowledgeable in your area of work, this obstacle is easily overcome and credibility gets attached to your name. When you are informed of latest trends in your field and industry, it becomes easier for you to attract people to follow your goals. Quite easily, half the battle is won this way. When people trust that you know your job well, they tend to agree with your recommendations, accept your judgments, and abide by your decisions.

The worst an administrative leader can do is to claim credit for another person's work. This puts your credibility at risk, declares you unworthy of trust, and damages your reputation. If you are not sure of something, do not say it. If you do say something, you have to follow through and do it.

As an example, you have intentions to promote a diligent and deserving employee this year. However, during the promotion exercise, you are asked to withdraw your nomination because your superior says there are others in the waiting list. Sounds familiar? What would you do if you encounter such an experience?

The right thing to do here would be to proceed as you had rightfully mentioned and put the employee up for promotion. The reason for this is simple: your boss may not know your employee well enough to make a sound judgement, but you know this person is deserving of a promotion. Furthermore, you have already given the employee your word. To this employee, your words mean something. You are his/her administrative leader and your credibility is now at stake.

Nominating this employee for a promotion may appear useless as it requires support from your superiors before it can go through to the next level, and you now know this person's application may be brushed aside. However, you have done your fair share and kept your word to this person. Whatever the outcome, your conscience is clear.

To add on, if you have already proven your own credibility in your company, your evaluation of this employee will be given due credit and weighed in with more importance as compared to others. As I mentioned earlier, people will tend to agree with your recommendations, accept your judgments, and abide by your decisions – all credit goes to your credibility!

Credible administrative leaders make decisions rationally and do not shift their focus abruptly. Though some may contest that such leadership is relatively predictable, being predictable to your own people as observed by your own behaviours is commendable and not detrimental. You may only want to be unpredictable to your competitors or closest rivals.

To gain more credibility, an administrative leader must practice open communication. It is proven that a responsive person is perceived to carry more credibility as compared to someone who is unresponsive. Being responsive is not just about being heard, but being felt. Your presence alone makes plenty of difference. Communicating and interacting via emails or/ and telecommunication modes may at times be inadequate to your followers, and you may mistakenly portray a shallow impression of yourself. To be credible as an administrative leader, you should make it a point to interact face-to-face (as much as possible).

As pointed out earlier, if you say something, you should do it. Do not blurt out empty words. Actually DO it - regardless of how tiny or massive a promise it is. All the small things we say but fail to do erode our credibility, causing more harm than we know. Administrative leaders with credibility are consistent in their words and behaviours. They never say one thing and do another.

There are countless watchful eyes keeping track of your credibility by gauging your actions against your expressed behavioural perceptions. It is a constant challenge to gain credibility, and once you have earned it, it is even harder to maintain that high level of credibility. I would relate credibility to a book – easy to buy but time-consuming to assimilate!

Often, many administrative leaders, particularly middle managers, start to stumble when they are caught in sensitive situations between their subordinates and superiors. There are situations that puts you in a dilemma when you need to choose between losing your credibility as a superior (with your subordinates) or gaining your credibility as a subordinate (with your superiors).

My advice to you is this: gain your own credibility with your superiors to get their support first before trying to appear credible to your subordinates. Whatever the situation may be, always remember it is far worse to lose your vision than to lose your sight. In application, never give up or compromise your credibility for small gains for there is nothing better by far than being credible!

5.2. *Communication*

If you cannot communicate, you are not an administrative leader. Communication, perhaps, is the deciding factor that determines your ability to lead and succeed. Lack of communication is the single leading cause for the annihilation of most relationships anywhere. Effective communication is essential for all aspects of life.

Communication is not merely talking, as many assume it to be. Communication can be termed as simple measures people do to succeed in conveying information to one another. It is a process meant for two or more to acquire certain information transmitted. This is so regardless of the method of transmission.

Frequently, many administrative leaders complain they are unable to communicate effectively. This problem could often arise due to the presence of external factors or simply because they do not know how to be communicative. The most vital step to succeed is to comprehend that communication is a two-way process. In a discussion, the person transmitting the message is the transmitter and the party receiving the message becomes the receiver.

Since communication is basically the transmitting and receiving of information, surely there are more than a single way of doing it. In fact, there are many different means of getting a single message across to someone. The employment of different tactics is necessary depending on the sort of message transmitted and the party receiving it.

Imagine an engineering lecturer using mathematical and engineering terms to teach a class filled with nursing students. It defeats the primary purpose of getting the information across to the audience effectively and efficiently. It disrupts the learning process and thus affects and disables proper communication from effectively taking place between the students and lecturer. To communicate, you must speak the same language as your audience. This is not always true. But it is mostly acceptable.

As such, communication must be adapted to suit the receiver. As an administrative leader, the first rule of communication is to know your colleagues and co-workers well. Each of them has different opinions of you and of the topic being communicated. Similarly, you would carry a different opinion of them and of the topic. How you communicate with them is based on how you perceive them and the topic as perceived by them.

You do not typically communicate with your audience like you would with your household. Communication in general should be inoffensive and acceptable to the receiving party. At times, much time is taken to realize this hard fact. It is similar to executing a presentation to a particular group of people – you would normally put in some effort to understand the audience you are presenting to so as to cater to their needs.

Another common error committed by administrative leaders is the inability to study the stumbling blocks to effective communication and understand the presence of barriers when communicating. Poor communicators are generally those who do not see subliminal messages, especially non-verbal clues and the body language of their listeners.

With close observation, you will be able to pick up the mental states of those involved in the communication process. When you seek to analyse the receiver (assuming you are the transmitter), you take your communication one step further by manipulating your communication style to cater accordingly. In doing so, you prevent a major communication breakdown that may eventually lead to misunderstandings, confusions, and missed targets/goals.

For example, your colleague or subordinate seems uncomfortable when you assign him/her a particular job for the day. You spot this discomfort and unease from the person's reluctance to spontaneously accept the task and you immediately sense that there is more than meets the eye. You realise there are only a couple of likely reasons for this reluctance - incompetency or unfamiliarity of the task assigned, and/or personal problems outside of work.

As an administrative leader, you choose your next course of action. You can now change your communication style to befit your receiver - see if you can address the root cause before getting back to assigning the task. For instance, if the employee's hesitance is due to incompetency or lack of skills, you might get him/her to understudy another person who is adept and skilful in this area, or provide training in such functional areas to boost competence levels.

If it is a personal problem, then you talk to the employee to see how you can best help them. Offer them your assistance and re-assign the work accordingly so that disruptions are minimized. By doing so, not only will you be seen as an effective communicator, but also regarded as an understanding leader.

An even greater challenge posed to an administrative leader is when it is necessary to deal with angry and dissatisfied clients or customers. This occurs frequently in a service environment. However, it is not just limited to the service industry. You may face angry bosses or dissatisfied subordinates too.

More often than not, an incompetent communicator is bothered by such circumstances. But remember, you have the power to change this situation around if you can handle the person (and the situation) well. When faced with such challenges, you may even be able to improve your relationship with the other, and create room for growth and more opportunities.

All you need to do is to listen not just with your ears but with your heart. Be empathetic (not just by words but be sure your body language shows this) and patient. Once they are done talking, you solve the problem if you can do so at once; and if you are unable to, always remember to follow up to close the loop. Most unhappy clients forget the incident when they walk away, but get more frustrated when their complaint is not taken seriously and followed up on. It is the same case for your superiors who get agitated only when you fail to follow up.

In a crisis situation, your communication skills are once again put to the test. Your usual methods of communication may be subject to failure and you, as an administrative leader, need to employ modified techniques to convey messages effectively and efficiently. As a rule of thumb, in such scenarios, avoid getting too objective with the end result and concentrate on getting the right messages across to the right people as soon as you can through the right channels. Use what methods (and resources) you have within your power to cascade information to all relevant parties.

Regardless of what your role in the organization could be - whether marketing, project management, service, events management, finance, human resource, corporate matters, or a complex mixture of more than one of the above, you can follow the simple steps in the next paragraph to communicate effectively and achieve your goals.

Before you begin to communicate for any purpose, remember to compose yourself. Be organized and have your aim and the end point clearly in mind. Understand your audience and tailor your communication according to their profile. Choose your mode of delivery (group meetings, presentations, emails, SMS) for transmitting and be receptive to feedback. Maintain an open mind, pay close attention to non-verbal clues and subliminal messages, and be ready to unlearn and relearn if needed. Lastly, do a decent follow up and close the loop where necessary.

Many claim spoken languages to be a huge barrier to communication. Spoken language is nothing but a bridge to transfer information. If communication can only be successful by speaking the same language, how then do inter-cultural weddings happen? It is amazing that people of different religions and languages can actually understand each other more than those sharing a common language. As surprising as this is, it is equally commendable.

Administrative leaders must be alert and aware of common factors that hinder communication. Anger, impatience, negligence, stress, fatigue and complacency are just a few to be named. Even the most clear and concise information would get distorted by the time it reaches the other end when the above-mentioned hindrances are overlooked or treated lightly.

Everyone in the world communicates. Each one of us is born with the natural ability to communicate effectively. Communication breakdown occurs only because we choose to disrupt this natural process of communicating.

Though different in many ways, we are all born similar in that we are blessed with the ability to communicate. We ought to utilize this in-born gift wisely. Because of miscommunication, countries go to war, economies collapse, and organizations fail. A true administrative leader is one who stands tall and sets exemplary standards in communication.

5.3. *Clarity*

Have you ever experienced a situation where you knew what you wanted, but just did not know how to say it? It is no surprise that clarity comes in as an important quality for an administrative leader. The preceding chapter on communication is closely related to clarity as well. Clarity, simply defined, refers to being clear and free of ambiguity. A quality of such importance brings about disastrous and severe implications if overlooked.

An administrative leader is clearly in command, regardless of the industry (s)he is in. Numerous instructions are passed down to fellow workers daily. In several incidents worldwide, blame has been apportioned to the lack of clarity or ambiguity of commands from people in places of authority.

It helps to ask how the incident happened and what can be done to prevent a recurrence of the same problem. Regardless of countless questions asked, the blame approach is unlikely to eradicate the aftermath of an incident. Incident reporting, revisiting document records, performing root cause analysis, writing preventive measures, and introducing new policies - all can follow but cannot redeem the damage that is already done in terms of both reputation and cost.

My advice to all administrative leaders in positions that require the frequent handing down of instructions is to cultivate the practise of having clearly defined Standard Operating Procedures (SOPs). SOPs explain in detail how a certain procedure should be carried out. SOPs are a daily feature of many high and low risk industries. Within the aviation industry, for instance, airline pilots unanimously concur that SOPs make flying safer.

The severe impact of not following SOPs, especially in high-risk industries, has resulted in catastrophes.

Drawing another example from the aviation industry, aerospace and aircraft maintenance engineers always are told to follow SOPs very strictly. Should they experience ambiguous instructions in the maintenance manual, they are to seek clarification from the aircraft or equipment manufacturers. Until such time as clarity is obtained, they are to cease all work. While some argue that a grounded aircraft results in loss of revenue, the safety of aircraft passengers cannot be compromised. SOPs dictate what employees are to do, when they are to do it, and how to do it. All they need to do then, is to follow the instructions!

Although people often resist at first, they quickly come to terms with SOPs once they realize that these are in place for a valid reason to ensure that work is being carried out in a proper manner, ensuring that no harm befalls any human or damage to equipment. SOPs actually provide a real opportunity to drive safety and improve working relations. More than that, SOPs provide much needed motivation and can boost worker confidence.

Across industries, resistance to the adoption of SOPs and their slow uptake is caused by barriers such as fear of uncertainty, lack of trust in written rules, ambiguity and lack of familiarity with guidelines, and lack of motivation to change existing practices. Resistance in most cases are minimal as people have begun comprehending the importance of SOPs. Many industries now spend millions of dollars to ensure adequate time is spent conducting training for all staff to help them understand SOPs and work procedures.

While there should be clarity in all instructions, an administrative leader's responsibilities are not limited to that. Sometimes it takes more than clearly defined SOPs. (S)He should also be able to demonstrate clarity in actions in things they (try to) do. This may appear less critical but is indeed a crucial factor. We shall take a look at the following example.

You are about to close a million dollar deal with a vendor who has been providing services to your organization. However, you suddenly realise that your department's allocated budget for this fiscal year is barely sufficient and as such, you prefer some cushioning to your budget moving forward.

In good conscience, you decide to negotiate with the vendors for a further discount. Abruptly, without realizing watchful eyes are on you, you request that your co-workers who are still in the meeting room leave the room immediately as you feel that negotiations are harder with more people around. This peculiar behaviour of yours could raise eyebrows!

Your intentions were good, but your actions lacked clarity. To a large extent, your actions may have even appeared controversial and misleading. As an administrative leader, transparency is very important. In this scenario, your actions will be easily misjudged and warrant unwanted attention, when all that you wanted was for the good of the organization and your people.

A more diplomatic and tactful approach in this case would be to mention to the vendors (in the presence of your co-workers) that you need some time to rethink their proposal. Soon after this, you could have asked your co-workers to leave the room so that their time can be better utilized.

In this way, there is less ambiguity to your action and less room for doubts and misinterpretation. In the above scenario, your colleagues would have been able to better appreciate the clarity, and therefore a better understanding of your intentions and the gravity of the situation.

A country prefers a government which is clear and considerate. A company prefers leaders whose intentions are crystal clear and who are able to chart visions, goals, and aims clearly. Never take clarity for granted, as such a minor quality as this can create problems too large to be easily handled at a later stage.

Clarity is as important an attribute in leaders as it is in a diamond – the clearer the gem, higher its market value. By the same token, the clearer the administrative leaders are, the higher they are valued.

5.4. *Control*

It is important that you, as an administrative leader, control every activity with prudence, by employing right tactics, and in a just manner. Too much control can kill your goals, harm your co-corkers, and ultimately affect your own performances. Too little control can cause you to lose focus, miss your timelines, and drift further from being able to lead and motivate an efficient team to achieve goals.

Control is a crucial part of managing. You should have proper control in everything you do if you intend to successfully achieve your outcomes, be it for your country or organization.

An administrative leader can never effectively manage without the capacity to control.

The act of controlling can be further segregated into finer elements - controlling resources, controlling activities, controlling results, and controlling damages. This is a continuous chain and will not yield positive results should the chain be broken at any point. The following picture (I term it the Circle of Control) illustrates the closely knitted relationship between the four elements.

As an administrative leader, your primary focus is to achieve positive results for your company, those around you, and yourself. The element of control plays a central role in your aspirations to steer your people and organization towards positive results.

Figure 3: Circle of Control

First, you need to start by having proper control over your resources. People are your greatest asset and resource. Controlling people here does not imply you use force or strike fear into them, but try controlling your people with the use of rewards, recognition, and appreciation. Get them to be a part of the overall vision and every success.

Share your achievements and give them credit where credit is due. Reward those around and with you consistently and fairly. Garner support from the people to lift all barriers that hinder you from achieving your aims and goals. Gather all available resources (hardware and software) and deploy them appropriately where they are required.

Second, once you have a good span of control over your resources (especially people), you can then start to drive the activities to reach a desired state (in order to fulfil intended or targeted objectives). Get the people to function for you in the way you would want them to. Push them objectively towards common goals and show them the way by walking the talk. Streamline administrative services and functions to everybody's advantage.

The people working on the ground would know the troubles encountered on the ground. Therefore, getting them to be a big part of any administrative reform makes perfect sense. In a matter of time, they would be able to guide you in the correct direction to achieve your goals with well evaluated and administered activities.

Third, once you have laid a strong foundation on the activities you need to carry out to achieve positive outcomes, you need to control the final results. Although many think of this phase as being the most important, it is what you do for the first two phases that really matter and that determines the success of this third phase. Even though the results may be self-driven to some extent once you have successfully completed the two initial phases, results should not be left totally unattended without any form of control. In short, there should be continued supervision without any intervention.

The last phase is what I would call 'a necessary evil'. Damage control will not be always needed, but in cases where you fail to achieve positive results, it might be required. All organizations, large and small, do this. In most cases, it is at this last phase that many tend to blunder.

Many failures become publicized and well known as a result of poor management, or simply put, poor damage control. As an administrative leader, you must be quick to respond to problems that surface and address such problems both internally and externally. A prompt response is usually indicative of your company's emphasis and proactivity levels on damage control, genuine attitude to correcting mistakes, and responsibility in accepting facts and facing truths.

Be transparent and open about what happened and the factors that allowed it to happen. Be frank in your response and mitigate any damages to reputation. Finally, conduct an After Action Review (AAR) and identify the root cause. Draft out long term plans and preventive measures, stay motivated, and move forward in a careful and positive manner.

Most administrative leaders misinterpret the term control and abuse it. Abusing your authority or over-controlling resources, people, activities, and even results, never makes you an exemplary leader. You must showcase yourself to be an administrative leader with a well-balanced control in all four mentioned phases and elements.

5.5. *Conflict Management*

There is a saying that a perfect match in marriage can only be found between a blind wife and a deaf husband. This is because a blind wife would not be able to observe the flaws and negative aspects of her husband while a deaf husband cannot hear his wife's daily nagging.

Taking reference from this analogy, some administrative leaders think they should act either blind or deaf. They even go further and believe this can work both ways between the leader and follower. Unfortunately, this is a common mistake an administrative leader can be guilty of and is never advisable.

In reality, disagreements happen to everyone. Disagreements are normal and a healthy sign. As long as two or more people are involved in an activity together, an argument can break out as you cannot expect them to agree on everything all the time. Even identical twins can share different opinions and this is an acceptable norm.

An administrative leader must admit that conflict is inevitable. Conflicts trigger negative emotions and can lead to anger, disappointment, and resentment - none of which does any good for you and those around you. Conflicts can also be an energy draining ordeal altogether. Administrative leaders commonly misunderstand conflict as the real problem when it is actually not.

Conflict is good at times as it introduces healthy competition, forces teams to promptly evolve through the stages of team dynamics (forming, storming, norming, and performing), and elevates constructive tension that produces better results. There are numerous benefits that may be gained when conflict is resolved in a healthy manner. The team will understand you better and vice versa, objectives will appear clearer, and with newly strengthened bonds, you, as an administrative leader, will achieve better results easily.

However, the toughest challenge for an administrative leader is to manage conflict. Very frequently, an administrative leader fails to negotiate for positive outcomes in a conflict due to poor management. The main reason being that our own temper gets in the way. Our emotions, disappointments and expectations manifest in a rage that can sometimes get out of hand. This fury destroys our targets, objectives, focus, forged relationships, and finally, it destroys us.

If you are unable to control your own feelings and emotions, how do you expect your co-workers and partners to treat and respect you as a leader? When you are stressed, you are mostly concerned about your own emotions and lose attention to many other factors that surround you, especially the intricate ones.

Failing to comprehend your own requirements, the chances are high that you would fail miserably in trying to understand what your co-workers need and feel. This leads to a communication breakdown resulting in disputes, mismanaged clients and services, lost profits and, in a larger magnitude, enmity among colleagues.

One common issue that gives rise to conflict at the workplace is when instructions are ambiguous and misaligned. An administrative leader should be clear when giving instructions. It is a good and effective practice to check back with receivers whether the information given was clearly and accurately understood. I hold regular meetings with my team members to ensure that work to be done for the day is complete, and work to be done for the next day is well and accurately understood.

Stress is another common factor leading to conflict. Usually, stress originates from heavy workload, personal problems, inadequate resources, unclear working relationships, and poor leadership. In such scenarios, the administrative leader must be patient, empathetic, and consultative. It is not enough to lend a listening ear, but you should understand the origin of the problem in order to completely dispel it.

I would normally pay close attention to the non-verbal clues given by the other party. I would then proceed to respond to the underlying issue that really stirred this conflict. In other words, I choose my responses more prudently and at the same time, get to the root cause of the problem.

To manage conflict effectively, the administrative leader should practice an 'open door' policy. When you sit close to your staff (not necessarily physically), you become a part of them. This simple act of yours will go a long way in helping to build trust and eliminate the existence of any strong hierarchical division between you and your staff.

Conflict that is poorly managed is much like a sophisticated time bomb - when it finally explodes, it destroys everyone around it. It is intricately designed and yet delicate. The effects are devastating and do much harm. In short, it kills and destroys all dreams, aspirations, aims and relationships.

An administrative leader's job is never to get imprisoned or entangled by conflict. Those are signs of eminent failures in your role as an administrative leader. Make tolerance, patience, accommodation, and acceptance your style of leadership and if possible, your way of life. Accept another person's perspectives, ideas, visions and behaviours the way they are presented.

5.6. Collaboration

There are many elements required to make a person successful. Among many other notable traits, one that stands firm and evidently distinct is the act of collaboration. Collaboration means to work in partnership or in simpler terms, working together in order to achieve a common goal.

For a business to be successful, it needs to collaborate with the right partner. For a country to flourish and prosper, collaborative effort among countries (especially neighbouring countries), and between the government and its citizens is required. Likewise, for administrative leadership to be successful, you need to collaborate effectively and appropriately with those around you.

If you are an administrative leader, you must understand and accept the truth that many activities in this world require collaborated effort in order to take place with ease. This holds true regardless of the scale, intensity, or magnitude of the activity. Often, a task of great complexity can be easily accomplished when the right hands are jointly handling it.

The Taj Mahal was not built by a single person. The idea to build Taj Mahal belonged to a king named Shajahan. He built it as a gift of love for his wife. Although the idea for such a wonder of the world to exist boiled down to one man's desire, it would never have been possible without the help of countless sculptors and workers (possibly slaves) who slogged day and night. This great magnificent structure still stands the test of time and against all odds thanks to a very successful collaboration.

Another example would be the Kailashnatha Temple in Ellora, Maharashtra. Today, it still is considered to be one of the greatest feats of engineering ever – uniquely carved out of a single stone (or even a mountain as some claim) from a top-down approach. The sculptors and engineers began by starting at the top of the rock and then carving their way straight down. Collaboration can lead to wonders.

Many administrative leaders are often reluctant to collaborate with other parties. I believe that the primary reasons for this are because: they think their ideas may be misinterpreted, they feel that they are off better working alone, or they see themselves losing control over the decision making process. However, it has been proven time and again that administrative leadership is very much dependent on adopting a collaborative attitude. Working together is extremely important.

By not collaborating, you stand to lose out more – amazing ideas that could be developed along the way by colleagues from another department are left unexplored, the likelihood of your work getting completed in time becomes questionable, and your business might lose out to existing stiff competition.

In the case of a country, there could be a major impact to the economy without collaboration. Many policies worldwide are based on best practices in any given field. Collaborations open doors to freedom of trade, exchange and exploration of foreign talent, cultivation and development of new knowledge, and even learning from mistakes.

There are countless complicated projects that could be underway in your organization and which will continue to be in the pipeline. Most of these projects may be dependent on many parties or stakeholders. By not collaborating, you soon reach a state of dilemma as the other stakeholders will gradually lose interest, ownership and commitment. When stakeholders eject in such cases, the losses are huge. You might even find yourself left stranded!

You become inundated with work by working alone even though you think you may be talented and extremely good at what you do. Everyone has limits and a breaking point. You may generally feel tenser due to a sudden increase in responsibility and workload. Furthermore, all these pile up on top of your routine work duties and commitments.

Mental stress and ill health effects often follow as a result. As an administrative leader, you could end up losing emotional balance and focus during this stage. The detrimental effects could likely cause you to lose sight of your vision, plans, and effectiveness at work and home.

Collaboration increases efficiency and reduces unwanted workload. An effective administrative leader is one who allows the workload to be equally and fairly distributed, but retains control over critical decisions made. It becomes your mandate to examine decisions that could be delegated to others to make. Basically, you need to delegate a certain level of authority to ensure continuity and consistency in work.

To attain a successful collaboration, you must first understand that each individual may generate different ideas. Your ideas may sometimes even contradict one another. To avoid any misunderstanding or confusion, you must be able to see the bigger picture and remind everyone on the team to stay focused on the end result. After a while, the thinking of the team will slowly but surely progress to the next level, making idea generation and problem solving a breeze.

The vision of all parties collaborating must be the same. Usually, the more parties required to collaborate, the more challenging it will be. So, it should be in the capacity of a capable administrative leader to closely collaborate with others without crossing boundaries, resolve conflicts when called for, and maintain efficacy.

As an administrative leader, you must be aware of the direction you wish to take and steer everyone on the team towards the same direction. The other advantage is that even if you get lost, your team is able to bring you back on track. As the spirit of efficient collaboration is achieved only after a storming stage for many, keep your sole purpose of getting to the end result as the driving factor. In no time, your team will start performing.

5.7. *Change*

Change is the only constant in life! Bringing about change in an organization is a difficult task. The challenge is magnified when working with a large and complex organization. As an administrative leader, you can tweak working procedures (or related SOPs) to quickly respond to a much needed change. However, many effective change agents have failed in trying to change the working environment.

Most administrative leaders tasked with driving change within an organization channel their energy and focus on fighting and defending the reason for the change. Unfortunately, the only thing tougher to change than change itself is the human mind-set. Facing objection and resistance is energy sapping and can detract from your goals.

You can never achieve a paradigm shift if you tell your employees why they need to change because you are focusing on the reason for change and not on what they stand to gain with the change. Many would agree that a much better approach is to redirect the attention of people to a higher value of what they want, by offering feasible solutions, different perspectives and useful insights. Magicians use this trick all the time – they get their audience to focus where they want them to focus on because that is what the audience desires.

People within a system are so accustomed to existing practices and will not be readily receptive towards a sudden change unless it benefits them. As much as your vision for the change is important, you need to put your peoples' needs before your own to drive the implementation plans for the change. The key principle to understand when you have to instil change in someone is that you cannot change them. They need to change themselves.

That is the primary reason why administrative leaders who are extremely effective change agents tend to focus more on offering solutions and addressing pain points of their people. By focusing on solutions rather than problems, you also see further ahead and envision the end state of the change you are implementing.

By now, we should all be on the same page, in unanimous agreement that leading change is no easy task, but it remains a necessity. In your own career, you will commonly be roped in to lead some kind of change. This change could be trivial or major, but the million dollar question is - how do you do it?

There is no one-size-fits-all solution when it comes to driving change within an organization. However, there are some general guidelines. A major change is often easier to implement if carried out in incremental stages rather than in its entirety. People tend to accept change better when they are progressively introduced to it.

The very first step you should take is to develop a project plan. A good project plan is one that states the vision and desired end state of the change, stakeholders affected by the change, detailed implementation schedule, communication plans, how you would manage the transitional phase in-between implementation, resource requirements, facilitation arrangements for the implementation, members of the project steering and sponsorship committees, activities with explicit details, risk mitigation plans for each activity, and consolidation and sustenance plans.

At a glance, the above list appears overwhelming but as you slowly work out the details, you will soon realize it is not as daunting as it seems. A prerequisite to implementing change is the ability to respond creatively to differences and to work towards mutual trust and understanding. Gaining the support of stakeholders is critical and success is already at the door once you clear this fundamental stage. At every step, it is pivotal that you have the stakeholders completely on board and not lose them. It is through them that you will be able to influence others who may not envision the benefits as well as you do.

As an administrative leader and change agent, you need to accept that people in a system see things differently. Getting everyone to see the same thing even though they are different is easier said than done. You need to steer everyone on board strategically in a course you desire and at the same time, ensure that they are able to clearly understand your vision and read your intentions. More importantly, they must constantly keep in sight of the ultimate vision of the change. Do not assume the perception of others to be aligned as further downstream in the course of change, people could get into disagreements due to a distorted vision of the change.

The interaction and understanding from stakeholders is critical to determine the need for change and to assess the present in terms of the desired future. In order to determine the changes to be made and to manage the transition, a one-time consolidation is often required. At this stage of change, you can review existing processes, filter value-adding processes from non-value adding ones, and obliterate those SOPs that offer no value.

This is a very crucial stage in implementing change as it helps you to see where you are, what you need to do, and how you get there to achieve your end objective of the intended change. Moreover, it allows you to study the resources you would need during your implementation, enabling adequate resource planning to be able to achieve your goals and meet timelines.

Success of any change is very much dependent on the manner in which it is implemented. If you as an administrative leader cannot visualize the end state of the change and the impact it can have on your people, you are highly unlikely to be able to chart out an effective project plan and implement change efficiently. How you initiate, drive and sustain change is a reflection of your qualities as an administrative leader. In other words, it is a sign of your capabilities to lead at present, and move on to accept larger responsibilities and portfolios in future.

You can relate change management to driving a car - if you do not know where to go or where you are at right now, you will not be able to reach your destination. No matter what you do, it does not take you long to realize that it is always a tough challenge to change the world for yourself, but it is much easier for you to change for the world. This is also the reason that efficient administrative leaders do not just concentrate on changing people, but are also willing to accept change for themselves as and when the need arises.

5.8. *Culture*

In any place, there will be a way things get done, a certain trend followed, or notably, a culture displayed. Oftentimes, how employees behave in an organization and why citizens of a country do things they do is set by the leader's culture. An administrative leader always has a culture and the culture is easily observed by looking at the followers. Culture is the way we do things.

Culture does not stand alone. There is no culture without administrative leaders as they are the people who actually drive it. Thus, the subject of administrative leadership is incomplete without the topic of culture. There are multiple reasons for people to undergo a change in culture or to adapt a new working style.

If you have noticed, in a large MNC, a variety of cultural differences can be observed. Since the employees of such MNCs could be from different countries, they bring along their own culture that they have followed for years. This is one instance in which cultural change may be called for.

Another instance when people may need to learn a new culture is when they change from one company to another. They may need to change their working styles to adapt to the new environment in the new company they have joined. Whether it is a national concern or a societal issue, it is the administrative leader's job now to introduce and inculcate a new culture. This is taxing but has to be done for the greater good. But how do you carry out such a mammoth task?

There are two issues here: first, you are trying to change an existing culture; and second, you are introducing a new culture. The administrative leader should be forthcoming to welcome other cultures first, so that people learn by using you as an example to embrace and cultivate a new culture. You should be explicitly clear with your company's goals, and set the benchmark for the need of a new or common culture.

This new culture the others are introduced to could be your own (your way of doing things). But most importantly, convince them to cross over to the new culture by justifying how it helps to achieve the targets and goals. Apart from objectives, teach them how your culture might make them more productive, and align them to their own career progression within the company. When you tell what they stand to gain, you provide them reasons to believe that the newly introduced culture is a proven method that delivers the best results, both for the company and themselves.

I once formed a new Integrated Student Services Centre (One Stop Centre). The team assigned to operate this Centre was transferred from different administrative departments. Since this new outfit was actually a consolidation of many administrative functions that were previously carried out by different departments, I had to guide them through the journey to unlearn and relearn not only new skills and knowledge, but an entirely new culture too.

As the person leading this Centre, they looked up to me to set the culture for them to follow – basically a new style of doing things that works for all of them. I constantly reminded them that the adage "Jack of all trades but master of none" no longer applics. My own version of the adage for them is "Jack of many trades and mastcr of at least one."

Another proven technique is to let them continue with their own culture first, and see if it works. This way, you earn their trust first, and should their culture fail to deliver the expected results, you now have the upper hand of the situation and should use that to your advantage to assure and persuade them to adopt the new culture.

Now you have your justification and reasons why your own culture works and you should have the support of your people. How do you go about spreading this culture that you want people to follow? There are three quick things you need to know and do if you wish to get there in a short span of time.

You begin by identifying the gaps between their present culture and where you want them to go. Next, you sieve out the common practices between their present and new culture. This filtering process will help you to identify what is amiss. Lastly, concentrate on providing adequate training - get them to undergo 'on the job' training by having them attached to people already well versed with your culture (if you already have people on the team).

By first identifying how far an individual is from the new culture, you set a pace that is required in introducing the new culture as you do not want to give this person (possibly a new employee) a 'culture shock'. When you sieve and filter out common practices, you are making your own life easier as you will eventually need to put in less work to mold this person (you only need to change what's different and not working). Finally, the best way to teach a new culture is by influence – getting someone who is accustomed to the new culture to impart. With a strong presence of an existing culture, it is easier to motivate someone to join hands to do things in a manner that proves to be effective.

You must remember that people learn beyond theories and principles. Once you get them to focus on how to apply theories in real-world cases and problems (application-based learning), you almost instantly achieve a win-win situation. They feel the need to quickly adapt to the newly learnt culture since it really works to provide results.

Finding a compromise between conflicting cultures is crucial to success. The biggest challenge in the next half-century is the spectrum of different groups with differing cultures and practices pulling organizations apart. Culture influences staff morale and attitudes of employees. It also has an indirect effect on a country's growth and economy.

It makes plenty of difference whether an employee in the organization is involved or committed to his/her work - involvement is ordinary but commitment is extraordinary. The degree of an employee's commitment is directly affected by the culture of the working environment, which in turn impacts the performance of the organization as a whole.

Hence, it is evident that a properly managed culture is extremely vital to form and promote committed service, improve standards and productivity. People are happier and function more effectively in a place with an established and accepted culture. As an administrative leader, you must be sure to seek common ground in a shared space and find a compromise among the many contradictions and different practices.

6. THE 'I' FACTORS

Administration-related job functions are often thought to be boring, mundane and unchallenging. Since most of us will be doing some kind of administrative work in some point of our career, it is helpful to appreciate works that are administrative in nature, rather than to approach such tasks with a fixated mind-set thinking they are monotonous.

It is natural for people to slow down, show less commitment, or at times a total lack of interest in jobs placing too much emphasis on administration. As such, it becomes the duty (and in some cases a challenge) of the administrative leader to convince people of the all-important administrative functions in any job. You as an administrative leader may believe in the power of administration, but how do you impart your beliefs and share your sentiments with your co-workers?

There are apparent ways to achieve this – through Imagination, Innovation, and Improvement. I call these the 'I' factors.

6.1. *Imagination*

Imagination can be described as the mind's ability to form known and unknown sensations without the use of senses like seeing, touching and hearing. All great ideas started from an imagination. I would like to perceive imagination as a sixth sense, and expect any capable administrative leader to imagine beyond boundaries.

The reality is that not all imagination will materialize due to unforeseen reasons. That, however, should never hinder you from imagining. When imagining, you expect never to fail. All brilliant ideas would have never succeeded should one have doubted the success of the imagination thereof. A good administrative leader never doubts his/her imagination to succeed, but should prepare for failures and do what it takes to mitigate risks.

Imagine if Walt Disney Productions never created the characters it now has – Mickey, Minnie, Donald, Daisy, and Goofy. This was a superb idea, but even before it became an idea, it was mere imagination. All these characters were formed by imagination. I personally like the following quote by Walt Disney;

"Disneyland will never be completed. It will continue to grow as long as there is imagination left in this world."

Walt Disney (American entrepreneur, cartoonist, animator, voice actor, and film producer, quote taken from Walt Disney's quotes – Brainy Quotes)

All success stories, big and small, began as a figment of someone's imagination. In fact, studies have shown that imagination helps make knowledge applicable in solving problems and is fundamental to integrating experience and the learning process.[14] So, it is of extreme importance that you imagine big as an administrative leader.

Never feel shy to express what you've imagined. You could have an imagination that can be worth exploring, and your idea makes administrative tasks interesting somehow. People may laugh at your imagination at first, but don't lose hope. Most importantly, work hard to convert your imagination to reality. Steve Jobs imagined putting a computer in every commoner's hands, and he did. I imagined authoring a book, and I just did!

6.2. *Innovation*

Some familiar synonyms of innovation would be transformation, restructuring, rearrangement, and alteration. My own definition of innovation is: to do the same thing in a new way. If the plan to attain a particular goal can be regarded as a strategy, the way you get there can be deemed as tactics. By innovating, you should not lose focus on your goal, but achieve the goal in another way. In brief, you maintain the strategy but alter your tactics.

An administrative leader who is innovative will think of redesigning existing workflows and processes in a less complicated and more objective manner. Non-value adding works should be dropped or eliminated totally if possible. The end result usually brings about a dramatic improvement in services, turnaround time, and customer satisfaction. The real gain lies in the radical paradigm shift in everyone's mind-set – administrative functions are not boring anymore! An innovative administrative leader will be able to make even the dullest jobs more colourful and shiny to those doing it. Start bringing innovation to your own work processes now.

6.3. *Improvement*

Improvement can be incremental or drastic. No matter what, improvement must be continuous. One should never become over confident as there will always be room for improvement. An effective administrative leader should think of what other improvements (s)he can continue to make.

In my opinion, improvement should become a daily norm and habit if you wish to stay successful. I tell people this: the moment you think you have achieved everything, is the moment your downfall begins. Look around, and it does not take you long to compile a long list of items, services, products, and even people you know that need improvement.

If you as a leader feel there's a much better way of doing a particular administrative task, you should do whatever it takes to have it improved. A good administrative leader believes in continuous improvement, and not just meeting objectives. Your colleagues, superiors, and subordinates will respect you for making improvements in a job function that make their working environment or their lives better.

"To be successful in a profession or business, to become wealthy cannot be compared to making the lives of your fellow men better."

Lee Kuan Yew (Singapore's First Prime Minister from 1959-1990, quote taken from Lee Kuan Yew quotes – Brainy Quotes)

Imagination-Innovation-Improvement

All the 'I' factors are actually linked and strongly connected to one another. This is easily explained.

The start point is always an idea formed by imagination. Through imagination, the seed of an idea gets planted. You now need to know how to execute it. To execute your imagination (and idea), you need to start innovating. Simply put, innovation is the process of planning and implementing your idea by assessing existing workflows, reengineering the steps, and revisiting procedures to create added value to customers, clients, and your own staff.

Finally, the improvement phase gives you the ability to measure, analyze, harness latest technology to gain competitive advantage, and optimize results. At the improvement stage, you would normally be looking into critical performance measures like cost savings, service standards, quality, and harmonizing staff working life. At any stage, you can revert to the imagination stage if you deem fit to do so.

It is not an easy task to change the existing impressions of many people around the world who think administrative tasks and related functions are boring and stagnant. However, with the successful application of the 'I' factors, I hope you are able to change that impression in due time.

7. DILIGENCE VS. INTELLIGENCE

This chapter explores and discusses two specific qualities - diligence and intelligence. This particular topic could open a can of worms and stir up much heated debate on whether an administrative leader needs more diligence or intelligence. However, upon closer scrutiny, you will soon begin to realize that when it comes to these two qualities, the catch lies not in how much of one you have over the other, but how much the lack of one over the other could reveal the vulnerabilities of the individual.

Diligence refers to hard work and conscientiousness, while intelligence can be defined as the capacity of an individual to comprehend problems and rationalize logically. There is indeed a huge difference between diligence and intelligence.

Every great invention came from a spark within - a sudden but promising idea that was implemented. Great scientists, researchers, inventors, engineers, entrepreneurs, and even politicians, have occasionally been regarded as symbols of brilliance when they clearly display one or several acts of intelligence in their own domain area, field, or industry. So, did they became successful due to intelligence (i.e. that spark from within)? Absolutely not!

Most renowned geniuses like Thomas Edison and Albert Einstein had similar sparks from within, a stroke of brilliance that came from nowhere. However, they did not succeed solely due to their brilliant idea nor superior intelligence, but due to their diligence in pursuing their idea till the end. Everyone successful, regardless of whichever field you draw an example from, succeeded due to their diligence in implementing their ideas, perseverance in wanting to achieve more, and living a life filled with dreams to better the lives of others around.

In educational institutions, academics routinely define students into two distinct categories – the "intelligent" and "others". It is assumed that the former group are those who have the ability to make the most complex problems look extremely easy. Rocket science to them is simple algebra. Only a few in this world fall under this category.

If all others were simply to fall under the latter category, then we are once again misled into thinking that human capacity is sadly limited. There is a very special category – the "diligent". Anyone can excel in anything when they are incomparably responsible, perseverant beyond measure, and willing to weather every pitfall that stands in their way. A diligent individual is one who strives hard, accepting stress and pressure, overcoming obstacles to achieve and stay on par with the "intelligent".

As far as administrative leadership is concerned, you would ideally have someone both extremely diligent and superbly intelligent. Unfortunately, the chances of finding such an individual are slim. An extremely diligent and rather intelligent person is a better choice as compared to a very intelligent individual who is just a little diligent. The reasons are simple.

A highly intelligent administrative leader would depend less on others as (s)he would feel that his/her decision is far superior to that of others', and that no additional consultation is required. Generally speaking, they believe less in collective wisdom, are more likely to be theoretical and idealistic, and show firm signs of dominancy in their leadership styles. They tend to be more authoritarian than others in their ways and mannerisms, as they believe that their thoughts travel faster than any other average individual.

A very diligent administrative leader, on the other hand, would involve the entire team as deemed appropriate in the decision making process. They generally believe more in collective wisdom, are more pragmatic in their approach to problem solving, and believe in application of theory. A diligent leader envisions, inspires, and influences followers to work cohesively towards common goals by gaining voluntary commitment over compliance. They achieve success by winning hearts and minds.

Though both diligent and intelligent leaders can promote creativity, support innovation, and draft a decent long term plan to achieve their visions, a very diligent leader would be more likely to achieve a better team bonding, inspire trust, pay more attention to details across the entire spectrum, and far exceed expectations in terms of management principles as compared to one who's intelligent (but less diligent).

Being a good administrative leader is less about being the smartest and more about understanding others and what makes a team work together to achieve solutions. As I said at the beginning of this chapter, the unique factor of these two qualities lies not in how much of one you have over the other, but how much the lack of one over the other could reveal the vulnerabilities of the individual. It is extremely important that you, as an administrative leader, are more diligent than intelligent. Having said that, do note that a severe lack of intelligence is a definite recipe for disaster and diligence alone cannot make up for this.

I have come up with the following Diligence vs. Intelligence Matrix. In the model, you will see the kind of leadership style you need to adopt and apply according to the quadrant you fall under in order to achieve success.

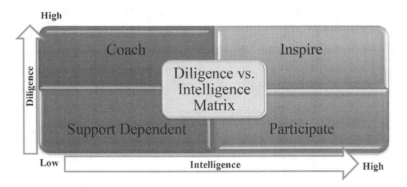

Figure 4: Diligence vs. Intelligence Matrix

For instance, if you are low in both diligence and intelligence, you will fall under the category of leaders who are Support Dependent – you will need to totally rely on external factors (your teams and others) to help you achieve your goals. Support dependent leaders are those who constantly come under immense pressure and have steep learning curves. They reach their positions due to circumstances or certain privileges and not because of their potential or competencies.

If you are high in diligence and low in intelligence, you will fall under the category of Coach – you may lack creativity and innovation, or sometimes the ability to quickly think on your feet. You should be ready to be coached by the intelligent ones (even if they are your subordinates) should the need arise as they may carry brighter ideas than you. Occasionally, you should be able to coach others on the ways of diligence in order to attain success as you probably rose to your position as a result of your hard work.

If you are high in intelligence and low in diligence, you will fall under the category of Participate – you need to learn how to participate in every activity carried out as a team so that you are able to better blend in to see better results. Intelligent leaders often share their bright ideas and leave the implementation to others. They often provide broad strokes from afar without 'getting their hands dirty'. To see a better outcome, such leaders should adopt a participative leadership style, staying close to the implementation team and at the same time sharing ideas and creative sparks with others to get everyone aligned to key objectives and the organization vision.

Finally, if you are high in both diligence and intelligence (a rare category), you will fall under the category of Inspire – all you need to do is simply to inspire your team, thus paving the way to great success! This is a very rare breed and only a handful of leaders out there are creative, bright, innovative, and also extremely diligent. Such leadership is often noted in entrepreneurs and politicians who have stood the test of time and withstood insurmountable challenges. Their names go down in history!

Diligent administrative leaders play a pivotal role in developing and integrating core strategies, enabling organizations to respond to the challenges of a fast-changing global economy to achieve their intended vision. They are also responsible for the planning, implementation, and management of policies and programs in their organization, as well as the development of services, technologies and applications in their respective areas of expertise and business. While intelligent leaders are sometimes needed to propose new ideas, diligent leaders are always needed to create a smooth administration and running of an organization!

8. CONCLUSION

Administrative leadership is so widely discussed in all corners of the globe, and yet the numerous theories and concepts explored have barely scraped the surface. Leaders exist on the basis that there are followers. Leadership is truly about giving, sharing and acting in the interests of those around. Real leadership never goes unnoticed. But all these are easier said than done.

There are some theories out there that argue that leaders reduce an individual's independency and bring about a decline in one's self-respect.[15] Nevertheless, most people actually prefer to be led than to be without a leader.[16] This "need for a leader" is especially strong in troubled groups that are experiencing some sort of conflict.[17]

Many others claim that leadership is an innate quality determined by distinctive characteristics coded within their DNA (e.g. intelligence, creativity, charm, charisma). However, there is evidence to show that leadership also develops through hard work and careful observation.[15] Effective leadership is a combination of nature (i.e. inborn talents) as well as nurture (i.e. acquired skills and knowledge).

It has been reiterated throughout the chapters that not all leaders are in managerial positions. A manager may have some command over what happens at work, but not necessarily the charisma to influence subordinates. Though leadership is certainly a form of power, it is not demarcated by power over people – rather, it is a power with people that exists as a reciprocal relationship between a leader and his/her followers.[15]

Contradictory to popular belief, the use of domination to influence others is never well-respected. Instead, leaders who adopt a consultative approach to achieve a common goal and strive to act in the best interests of others command better respect. All leaders must maintain a fine balance.

Though there are several examples out there to show that an authoritarian system can bring prosperity to countries and organizations, there is ample proof showing that such legacies may be ill-suited for 21st century challenges.

21st century administrative leaders must be able to lead with a vision. They must be able to inspire with a motive, influence with their charisma, and achieve desired outputs - no matter what that goal is. I would say administration is a key pillar and backbone of any successful organization or country. Without the presence of administrative leadership, plans to succeed can be easily derailed and go unimplemented.

Years of development and growth have brought about new paradigm shifts regarding the need for new central administrative functions regardless of an organization's core business or size. Administrative functions lead to the formation of new administrative departments. An administrative leader with wisdom and vision recognizes the need to take stock of many of these functions to better integrate them to meet the company's corporate objectives.

An administrative leader is one that aims to streamline decision making, improve response time and empower staff to manage and operate effectively and efficiently. Through proper consultation and clever analysis, (s)he achieves administrative excellence by simplifying complex workflows and creating collegiality, which in turn leads to various units within the same organization working collaboratively.

A sound administrative leader will be able to see far ahead, recognise that a strong administration is needed to enable the organization to function strategically, and enhance the roles of everyone within the organization.

Leaders of the present are faced with insurmountable demands and challenges as compared with previous eras. With new expectations, leaders of today have to deal with issues far more complex than before. Those who stand up to the challenges will inevitably either conquer or be conquered. Today, the world needs leaders who will walk with their followers, and not just point them in the right direction.

Some think that leadership can be easily cultivated, while others assume leadership is all about following the steps of successful people around. No matter what has been thought and assumed for ages, it is explicitly clear that a true leader takes pride in being unique and walks a path unexplored by another with conviction. This is only achieved by the relentless pursuit of excellence in everything that is done. A true administrative leader is one that leaves a legacy, even while yet alive.

On this road to unveiling and experiencing sound administrative leadership, wise and genuine leaders are those who discover their life's purpose and understand fully the big picture, without losing sight of the finer pieces that contribute to the bigger picture. Anyone, once they see where they fit in and understands their position, can and will become a true administrative leader. The era of The 21st Century Administrative Leader begins with this book.

9. REFERENCES

1. Bennis. W. 2007. The challenges of leadership in the modern world. *American Psychologist.* 62(1): 2-5.
2. Van Vugt, M., Hogan, R., & Kaiser, R. B. 2008. Leadership, Followership, and Evolution. *American Psychologist.* 63 (3): 182-196.
3. Bass, B.M. 2008. *The Bass Handbook of Leadership: Theory, Research, & Managerial Applications.* New York: Free Press.
4. Howell, Jon P. (2012). *Snapshots of Great Leadership.* London, GBR: Taylor and Francis. pp. 4–6. ISBN 9780203103210.
5. http://www.iias-iisa.org/groups/study-groups/sg-viii-administrative-leadership/administrative-leadership-description-research-agenda.
6. Gardner, J. W. (1965). *Self-Renewal: The Individual and the Innovative Society.* New York: Harper and Row.
7. Bennis, W. G. (1975). *Where have all the leaders gone?* Washington, DC: Federal Executive Institute.
8. Cecil A Gibb (1970). *Leadership (Handbook of Social Psychology).* Reading, Mass.: Addison-Wesley. pp. 884–89. ISBN 9780140805178. OCLC 174777513.

9. Hoyle, John R. *Leadership and Futuring: Making Visions Happen.* Thousand Oaks, CA: Corwin Press, Inc., 1995.
10. J. Nightingale (2008). *Think Smart - Act Smart: Avoiding The Business Mistakes That Even Intelligent People Make.* John Wiley & Sons. p. 1. ISBN 9780470224366.
11. https://osha.europa.eu/en/publications/reports/211.
12. Mehta, Harit (18 September 2011). "On Race Course road?". *The Times of India.* Archived from the original on 30 January 2014.
13. http://www.socialmediaexaminer.com/SocialMediaMarketingIndustryReport2014.pdf
14. Kieran Egan 1992, pp. 50
15. Forsyth, D. R. (2009). *Group dynamics* (5ᵗʰ ed.). Pacific Grove, CA: Brooks/Cole.
16. Berkowitz, L. (1953). "Sharing leadership in small, decision-making groups". *Journal of Abnormal and Social Psychology, 48,* 231–238.
17. Stewart, G. L., & Manz, C. C. (1995). "Leadership for self-managing work teams: A typology and integrative model". *Human Relations, 48,* 747 – 770.

Printed in the United States
By Bookmasters